A BEAR AFFAIR
Designs by Karen Sloan

Published by Provo Craft
Provo, Utah
Managing Editor, Clella Gustin
Design and Book Coordinator, Barbara Sanderson

Photography by Craig Young

For your convenience, Provo Craft computer numbers have been listed. Warehouse orders may be placed at the Provo Craft Warehouse, 1-800-937-7686, 285 East 900 South, Provo, Utah 84606. If you do not have a wholesale account, you may order retail from the Provo Craft Shipping Department at 1-800-563-8679, 295 West Center Street, Provo, Utah 84601.

Alternate wood sources for wood not cut by Provo Craft are A & P Craft Supply, 1-800-748-5090, 850 West 200 South, Lindon, Utah 84042, and Hansens' Wood Crafts, 1-801-227-7189, 460 East 1070 South, Orem, Utah 84097.

Provo Craft will make every effort to maintain an inventory of those wood items shown in our books; however, we cannot guarantee that they will be available for the sale life of the book.

TABLE OF CONTENTS

NELLIE NAPKIN HOLDER
This wood is not available through Provo Craft

PALETTE:
DECOART AMERICANA

Flesh Tone	Sable Brown	Moon Yellow	Buttermilk
Burgundy Wine	White Wash	Toffee	Lamp Black
Antique Gold	Jade Green	Raspberry	Dusty Rose

WOODCUTTING HINTS: The bear and back support are cut from 3/4" wood. Cut two 1/4" dowels 6" long. The overall finished size is 8 1/2" x 4 3/4".

WOOD PREPARATION: Sand and seal the wood.

PAINTING INSTRUCTIONS:
1. Toffee: Base the bear.
2. Flesh Tone: Base the dress and flower on the top of the head.
3. Buttermilk: Base the collar. Float highlights on the sleeves and paws. Lightly stipple highlights on the center of the dress skirt and the legs and feet.
4. Moon Yellow: Base the dress border. Dot the flowers on the dress. Base the back support.
5. Raspberry: Base the nose. Dry blush the cheeks. Stipple the flower center on the head.
6. Antique Gold: Float shade on the border.
7. Dusty Rose: Float shade on the dress.
8. Flesh Tone: Line the center line of the plaid on the dress border and back support. Base the flowers on the back support.
9. Jade Green: Base the leaves. Line the plaid lines on each side of the pink plaid lines on the dress border and back support, line the rick rack on the collar, the edge of the sleeves and the top of the dress border.
10. Sable Brown: Float shading on the bear's head, ears, hands, legs and feet.
11. Burgundy Wine: Float shade on the nose.
12. Toffee: Float shade on the collar.
13. Black: Dot the eyes. Very lightly spatter the entire piece.
14. White Wash: Dot the cheeks. Line the flower on the head. Dot the flowers on the back support. Very lightly float highlight on the nose and spatter the entire piece.

Finish: Outline everything with a permanent black lining pen. Glue the dowels into holes in the back of the bear and slide the back support into place.

VALENTINE GARLAND
This wood is not available through Provo Craft

PALETTE:
DECOART AMERICANA

Toffee	Raspberry	Burgundy Wine
White Wash	Lamp Black	Sable Brown

SUPPLIES:
6 Eye Screws
Scraps of Fabric (for bows) 2" x 6" cut 2, 2" x 12" cut 2.
Stencil # 41-5089 Checks, Hearts and Dots
19 Gauge Black Steel Wire

WOODCUTTING HINTS: All pieces are cut from 1/2" wood. The overall finished size of each piece is 3 1/4"x 4 3/4".

WOOD PREPARATION: Sand and seal the wood.

PAINTING INSTRUCTIONS:
1. Toffee: Base the bears.
2. Burgundy Wine: Base the hearts.
3. Sable Brown: Float shade on the bears.
4. White Wash: Stencil the dots, hearts and checks on the hearts. Stipple highlights on the bears' feet, hands, ears and center of each heart.
5. Raspberry: Base the nose. Dry blush the cheeks.
6. Burgundy Wine: Float shade on the nose.
7. Black: Dot the eyes. Spatter lightly.
8. White Wash: Dot the cheeks and highlight the nose. Spatter lightly.

Finish: Outline everything with a permanent black lining pen. Attach screw eyes to the bears and tie the bears together with wire and fabric bows.

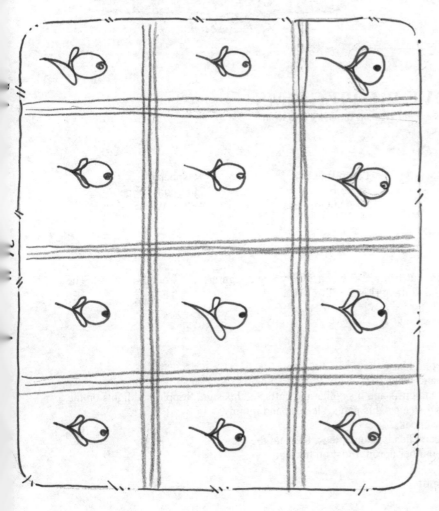

½ " wood

I LOVE PIE PILGRIMS
This wood is not available through Provo Craft

PALETTE:
DECOART AMERICANA

Jade Green	Avocado	Lamp Black	Raspberry
Toffee	Light Buttermilk	Sable Brown	Burgundy Wine
Evergreen	Slate Grey	French Grey Blue	White Wash

SUPPLIES:
19 Gauge Wire

WOODCUTTING HINTS: The pilgrims are cut from 3/4" wood. The pie and sign are cut from 1/4" wood. The overall finished size of the boy is 8 1/2" x 7" and the girl is 8 1/2" x 4 1/2".

WOOD PREPARATION: Sand and seal the wood.

PAINTING INSTRUCTIONS:
1. Toffee: Base the bears' heads, hands, feet and base the pie.
2. Jade Green: Base her dress and his shirt and pants.
3. Light Buttermilk: Base her apron, collar and cuffs and his collar and cuffs and his sign. Stipple highlights on the pie center, bottom of the dress, bodice and sleeves, his pants, sleeves, and tummy.
4. Raspberry: Base the noses. Dry blush the cheeks.
5. Sable Brown: Float shade on the bears' ears, heads, hands, legs, feet and the pie.
6. Toffee: Float shade on the collars, cuffs and her apron. Float on his sign.
7. Slate Grey: Base the pie tin.
8. French Grey Blue: Float shade on the pie tin.

9. Burgundy Wine: Float shade on the noses.
10. Jade Green: Line plaid on his collar and her pocket.
11. Evergreen: Line the bows and words on his sign.
12. Avocado: Float shade on her dress and his shirt and pants.
13. Lamp Black: Dot the eyes and spatter lightly.

14. White Wash: Dot the cheeks and spatter lightly. Float highlights on the noses. Stipple the center of the pie tin.

Finish: Outline everything with a permanent black lining pen. Wire the sign and pie to the bears as shown.

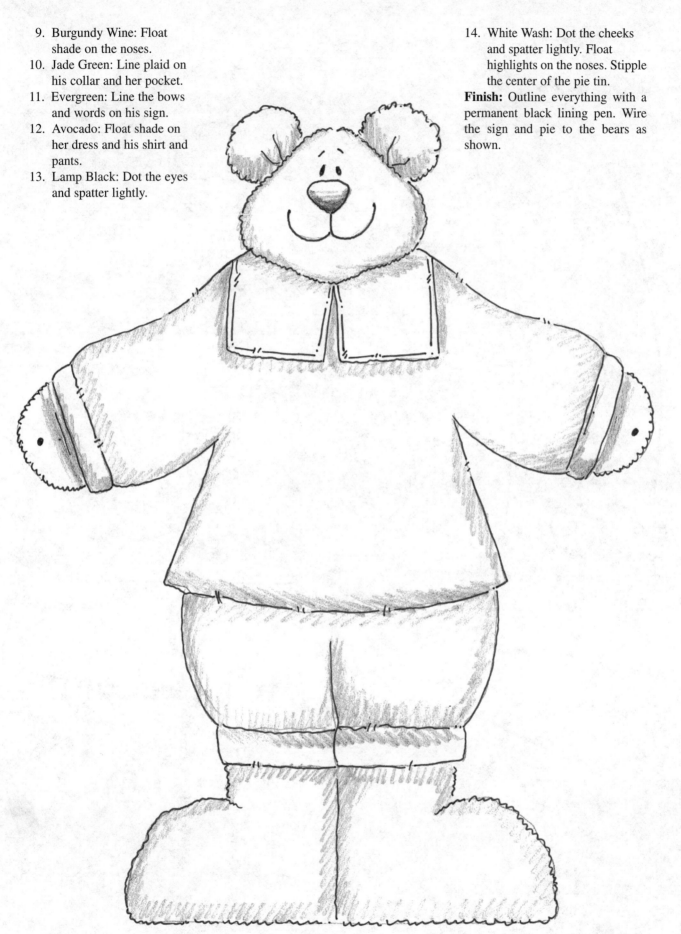

I Luv Pie

¼" Baltic Birch Plywood

PRISSY PILGRIM BOOK

PALETTE:
DECOART AMERICANA

Antique White	Buttermilk	Baby Blue	Burgundy Wine
Raspberry	White Wash	Dusty Rose	Evergreen
French Grey Blue	Deep Midnight Blue	Jade Green	Sable Brown
Lamp Black			

SUPPLIES:
31-0063 Paper Mache Book Box Set 4 3/4" x 6 1/2".

PAINTING INSTRUCTIONS:

1. Antique White: Base the book front, spine, and back cover.
2. Buttermilk: Base the pages and oval on the front cover.
3. Antique White: Base the bear's face and ears.
4. Baby Blue: Base the top of her cap and her dress.
5. Sable Brown: Float shade around the outside of the book and the oval, around the binding on the spine of the book and around the back cover of the book. Shade the ears and head of the bear and lightly around the bear's ears and head on the hat brim.
6. Dusty Rose: Base the flowers and dot the buds.
7. Raspberry: Base the nose. Dry blush the cheeks. Stipple the flower centers.
8. Jade Green: Base the leaves.
9. Evergreen: Float shade on larger leaves and stroke the center line and stem.
10. Burgundy Wine: Float shade on the nose.
11. White Wash: Stipple the highlight on the flower petals. Dot the flower centers. Line the plaid on the dress. Darken squares where lines connect. Dot the cheeks and cap.
12. Deep Midnight Blue: Line the bow at the collar.
13. French Grey Blue: Float shade on the cap and dress. Stroke highlights on the bow.
14. Black: Spatter everything lightly. Dot the eyes.

Finish: Outline everything with a permanent black lining pen.

LIBERTY BEAR
11-1944 Liberty Bears

PALETTE:
DECOART AMERICANA

Toffee	Buttermilk	Raspberry	Lamp Black
Deep Midnight Blue	Sable Brown	Burgundy Wine	White Wash

SUPPLIES:

.1 Black Pen   19 Gauge Wire

WOODCUTTING HINTS: Cut the pieces from 3/4" wood. The overall finished size is 7" x 6".

WOOD PREPARATION: Sand and seal the wood.

PAINTING INSTRUCTIONS:

1. Toffee: Base the bear.
2. Buttermilk: Base the shorts and right side of the star. Stipple highlights on the ears, arms, tummy and feet.
3. Raspberry: Base the nose. Stipple the cheeks.
4. Burgundy Wine: Base the stripes on the star and pocket. Float shade on the nose.
5. Deep Midnight Blue: Base the left side of the star and the small stars on the shorts. Dot the button on the strap.
6. Sable Brown: Float shade on the bear's ears, head, arms, tummy, feet, tail and legs and on the shorts around the pocket, crotch and strap.
8. Burgandy Wine: Dot the shorts.
9. White Wash: Stipple highlights on the stripes on the large star. Dot the blue side of the star. Dot the cheeks. Float a highlight on the nose. Dot the button on his strap. Spatter both pieces.
10. Lamp Black: Dot the mouth and eyes. Spatter both pieces.

Finish: Line everything with a permanent black lining pen. Curl a piece of wire and attach to the star and hand as shown in the picture.

10

WITCH BEAR?

11-1949 Witch Bear Med J/L

PALETTE:
DECOART AMERICANA

Toffee	Burnt Orange	White Wash	Antique Gold	Lamp Black
Jade Green	Moon Yellow	Buttermilk	Sable Brown	Light Cinnamon
Evergreen	Slate Grey	Raspberry	Burgundy Wine	

WOODCUTTING HINTS: The wood piece is cut from 1/2" wood. The overall finished size is 6 1/4" x 6 1/2".

WOOD PREPARATION: Sand and seal the wood.

PAINTING INSTRUCTIONS:

1. Toffee: Base the head and hand.
2. Jade Green: Base the dress and leaf.
3. Moon Yellow: Base the hat band and border of the dress. Float highlights on the leaf. Stipple the center of the dress and sleeve.
4. Burnt Orange: Base the pumpkin.
5. Lamp Ebony Black: Base the hat and shoe.
6. Sable Brown: Float shade on the ears, head and hand. Base the stem.
7. Light Cinnamon: Float the stem.
8. Jade Green: Line plaid lines on the dress border.
9. Evergreen: Float shade on the dress and leaf. Dot the hatband. Paint checks where the plaid lines cross on the dress border.
10. Moon Yellow: Stipple the pumpkin and lightly stipple the center of the stem.
11. Raspberry: Base the nose. Dry blush the cheeks.
12. Burgundy Wine: Float shade on the nose.
13. Slate Grey: Lightly stipple the top of the hat and the inside of the hat brim. Line the hat brim. Comma stroke and dot the top of the hat. Stipple the toe of the shoes.
14. Buttermilk: Float highlights on the ears, hand and pumpkin stem.
15. White Wash: Dot the cheeks. Dot the squares in the plaid. Float the highlight on the nose. Spatter the piece.
16. Antique Gold: Shade the border of the dress and the hatband.
17. Black: Spatter the piece. Dot the eyes.

Finish: Line everything with a permanent black lining pen as shown in the picture.

12

HANDY WIPERS TOWEL HOLDER
This wood is not available through Provo Craft

PALETTE:
DECOART AMERICANA

Toffee	Moon Yellow	Buttermilk	Antique Gold	Shale Green
Sable Brown	Raspberry	Burgundy Wine	White Wash	Avocado

SUPPLIES: 19 Gauge Wire   Heart Stencil

WOODCUTTING HINTS: The bear and base are cut from 3/4" wood. The towel is 3/8" wood. The dowel is 1/2" wide and 12" long. The overall finished size is 13" x 7 1/2".

WOOD PREPARATION: Sand and seal the wood.

PAINTING INSTRUCTIONS:
1. Toffee: Base the bear.
2. Shale Green: Base the base and the handy wipers towel, the leaves on the head, and the dowel.
3. Buttermilk: Base the collar and border of the dress. Stencil hearts on the outside edges of the base.
4. Moon Yellow: Line the plaid on the towel and the top of the base. Base the dress and flower.

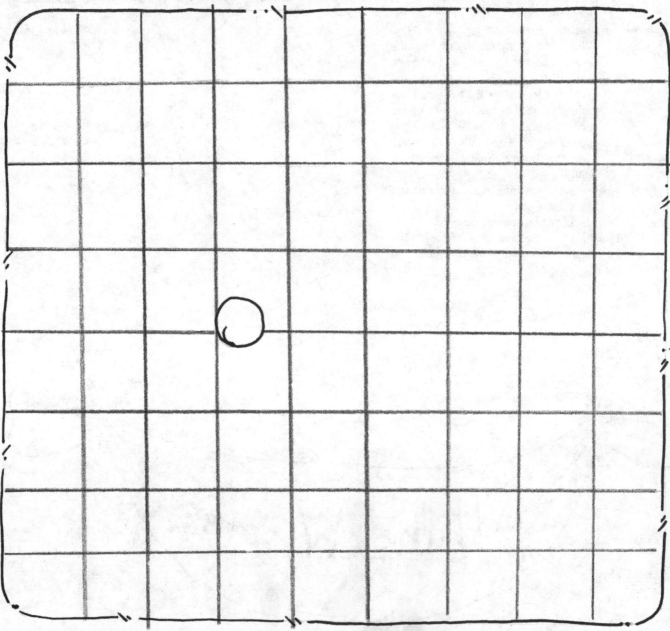

3/4" Wood

5. Shale Green: Line stripes on the dress and rick rack on the edge of the sleeves, top of the border, and collar. Stencil hearts on the border of the dress.

6. Antique Gold: Float shade on the dress.

7. Sable Brown: Float shade on the bear's ears, head, hands, legs and feet. Darken the shading on the edge of the skirt under the sleeves and on the bottom outside edges of the sleeves.

8. Toffee: Float shade on the collar and dress border.

9. Avocado: Float shade on the base and towel.

10. Raspberry: Base the nose. Dry blush the cheeks.

11. Burgundy Wine: Float shade on the nose.

12. White Wash: Stipple lightly on the sleeves and tummy area of the dress, bear's legs and feet, ears, hands and towel. Dot the cheeks and buttons. Float highlights on the nose, bottom of the collar, bottom of the border and the top edge of the towel and ends of the towel. Line the flower. Spatter everything lightly.

13. Outline everything with a permanent black lining pen.

14. Black: Spatter and dot the eyes.

Finish: Screw the bear onto the base. Wire the towel to each hand. Glue the dowel into the base.

3/4" WOOD

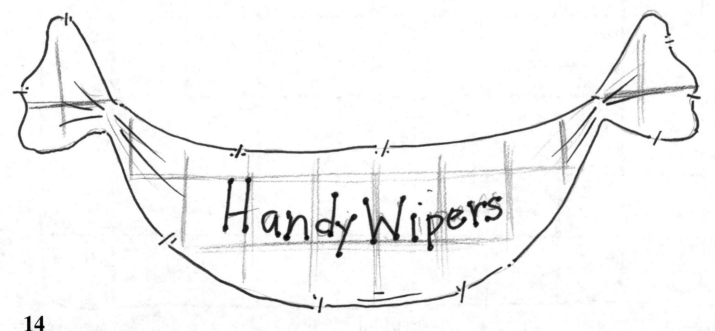

Handy Wipers

14

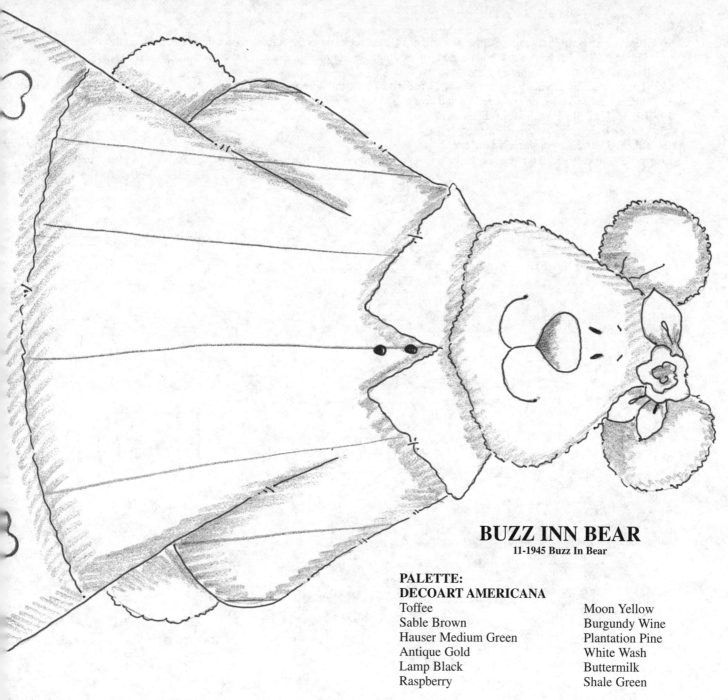

BUZZ INN BEAR
11-1945 Buzz In Bear

PALETTE:
DECOART AMERICANA

Toffee	Moon Yellow
Sable Brown	Burgundy Wine
Hauser Medium Green	Plantation Pine
Antique Gold	White Wash
Lamp Black	Buttermilk
Raspberry	Shale Green

SUPPLIES:

Black Pen   Water Base Varnish

WOODCUTTING HINTS: The bear and honey crock are cut from 3/4" wood. The bees are 1/8" baltic birch plywood. The overall finished size is 8 1/2" x 6 1/2".

WOOD PREPARATION: Sand and seal the wood.

PAINTING INSTRUCTIONS:
 1. Toffee: Base the head, hands, feet and crock.
 2. Hauser Medium Green: Base the overalls.
 3. Moon Yellow: Base the beehive and bees' bodies.
 4. Shale Green: Base the shirt and ladle in the crock.
 5. Sable Brown: Float shade on the ears, head, hands, feet and on the crock. Base the outside edges of the crock.
 6. Raspberry: Dry blush the cheeks. Base the nose.
 7. Antique Gold: Float shade on the beehive and bees' bodies. Base the honey on the top of the crock.
 8. Plantation Pine: Float shade on the overalls.
 9. Lamp Black: Base the bees' heads, stripes and hole in the beehive. Dot the eyes.

10. Buttermilk: Base the wings. Stipple the center of the crock, muzzle, hands, feet, top of the ears, center of the sections of the beehive, bees' bodies, and top of the ladle. Stipple the center of the overall legs and straps.
11. Burgundy Wine: Float shade on the nose.
12. Hauser Medium Green: Float the handle of the ladle. Line the lettering on the crock.
13. White Wash: Cross hatch on beehive and crock. Spatter the pieces. Highlight the honey and the bear's nose.
14. Toffee: Line plaid on the shirt. Float shade on the bees' wings.
15. Outline everything with black pen.
16. Black: Spatter the pieces. Dot the eyes.

Finish: Glue the crock to the legs of the bear and one bee on the shoulder, foot and crock. Varnish with water base Satin Varnish.

HONEY

3/4" Wood

1/4" Baltic Birch

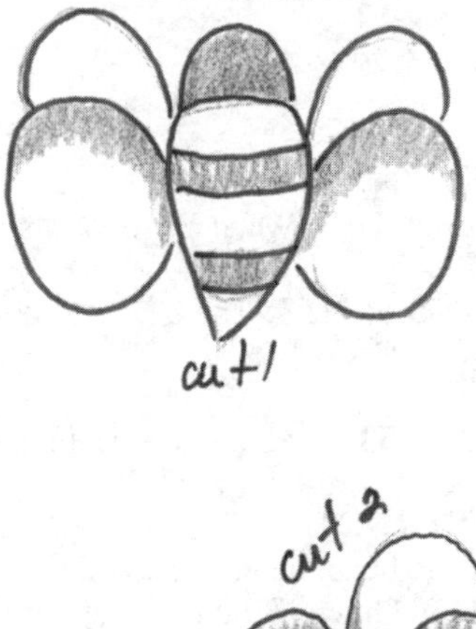

cut 1

cut 2

1/4" Baltic Birch Plywood

3/4" Wood

HO HO CHRISTMAS CARD HOLDER
11-1947 Ho Ho Card Holder

PALETTE:
DECOART AMERICANA

Hauser Medium Green	Hauser Light Green	Plantation Pine	Lamp Black
White Wash	Raspberry	Shale Green	Burgundy Wine
Antique Maroon	Buttermilk	Sable Brown	Toffee
Antique Green			

SUPPLIES:
Stencil #41-5089 Checks, Hearts and Dots

WOODCUTTING HINTS: All the wood pieces are cut from 3/4" wood. The overall finished size is 12 1/2" x 9 3/4".

WOOD PREPARATION: Sand and seal the wood.

PAINTING INSTRUCTIONS:
1. Hauser Light Green: Base the tree on the right.
2. Hauser Medium Green: Base the middle tree. Float shade on the light green tree.
3. Plantation Pine: Base the tree on the left. Float shade on the middle tree.
4. White Wash: Base the bear and base.
5. Shale Green: Base the sack.
6. Raspberry: Base the nose. Dry brush the cheeks.
7. Burgundy Wine: Base the hat and coat. Float shading on the nose.
8. Buttermilk: Base the fur on the hat and coat. Stipple the center of the sack, and top of the hat. Stencil dots on the coat and hat.
9. Toffee: Float shade on the bear's head, hands, legs and feet. Float shade on the front edge of the base.
10. Sable Brown: Float shade on the fur on the cap and coat.
11. Antique Green: Float shade on the sack.
12. Antique Maroon: Float shade on the coat and hat.
13. Black: Dot the eyes and spatter the bear and sack lightly.
14. White Wash: Lightly spatter all the pieces. Dot the cheeks. Float highlights on the coat, nose and cap.

Finish: Outline with a black lining pen. Screw the trees and bear onto the base.

BEE MINE CANDY BOX

PALETTE:
DECOART AMERICANA

Buttermilk	Toffee	Cranberry Wine	White Wash
Moon Yellow	Lamp Black	Raspberry	Burgundy Wine
Antique Gold	Sable Brown		

SUPPLIES:
Small Oval Paper Mache Box (31-2702, Set of five paper mache boxes - this pattern will fit the smallest box of this set. The approximate size is 7 1/2" x 5 1/4".)

Repeat from here for other side

Repeat from here for other side

18

PAINTING INSTRUCTIONS:

1. Buttermilk: Base the box lid, including the outside edge.
2. Burgundy Wine: Base the bottom of the box and the heart. Base the stripes on the side of the lid.
3. Toffee: Base the bear's head, hands, and feet. Float shade around the edge of the lid and side edge.
4. Sable Brown: Float shade on the bear's ears, head, hands, legs and feet and darken the shading around the edges of the lid.
5. Cranberry Wine: Float shade on the heart.
6. White Wash: Stipple the center of the heart, on the paws, ears and feet lightly. Line the word "Mine" and stitches for the bee trail.
7. Moon Yellow: Base the bee body .
8. Antique Gold: Float around the bee body.
9. Raspberry: Base the nose. Dry blush the cheeks.
10. Lamp Black: Line the stripes on the bee. Dot the eyes. Spatter lightly on the top only.
11. White Wash: Wash the bees' wings. Highlight the bear's nose. Dot the bear's cheeks. Spatter lightly on the top and sides of the box.
12. Outline everything with a permanent black lining pen.

WINTER MITTENS
11-1946 Winter Mittens

PALETTE:
DECOART AMERICANA

Deep Midnight Blue	Baby Blue	White Wash	Black	Buttermilk
Toffee	Sable Brown	Raspberry	Burgundy Wine	French Grey Blue

SUPPLIES: 19 Gauge Wire

WOODCUTTING HINTS: The mittens are cut from 3/4" wood. The overall finished size of each mitten is 3 1/2" x 5".

WOOD PREPARATION: Sand and seal the wood.

PAINTING INSTRUCTIONS:

1. Deep Midnight Blue: Base the mittens around the pattern of the bear.
2. White Wash: Base the bear.
3. Buttermilk: Base the fur on the mitten and the hat.
4. Baby Blue: Base the cap and bow.
5. Toffee: Float shade on the bear.
6. Sable Brown: Float shade on all the fur.
7. White Wash: Line the stripes on the bow and cap. Dot on the bow and cap. (Use the colored picture as a guide.)
8. French Grey Blue: Float shade on the bow and cap.
9. Raspberry: Base the nose. Dry blush the cheeks.
10. Burgundy Wine: Float the nose.
11. White Wash: Dot snow on the mittens and line and dot the snowflakes. Spatter the mittens.
12. Black: Dot the eyes. Spatter the mittens.
Finish: Outline everything with a permanent black lining pen. Curl the wire and attach the ends to the mittens.

3/4" Wood Cut 2

HAPPY HALLOWEEN BEAR
This wood is not available through Provo Craft

PALETTE:
DECOART AMERICANA

Toffee	Sable Brown	Black	Burgundy Wine	Jade Green
Light Avocado	Burnt Orange	Moon Yellow	Antique Gold	Buttermilk
White Wash	Raspberry	Brandy Wine		

WOODCUTTING HINTS: The piece is cut from 3/4" wood. The overall finished size is 4 3/4" x 3 1/4".

WOOD PREPARATION: Sand and seal the wood.

PAINTING INSTRUCTIONS:

1. Toffee: Base the bear's head, hands and feet.
2. Burnt Orange: Base the pumpkin.
3. Jade Green: Base the leaves.
4. Raspberry: Base the nose. Dry blush the cheeks.
5. Moon Yellow: Base the pumpkin's eyes and mouth. Stipple highlights on the pumpkin.
6. White Wash: Base the teeth on the pumpkin. Float highlights on the bear's nose and dot his cheeks.
7. Sable Brown: Float shade on the ears, face, hands and feet. Base the stem of the pumpkin.
8. Burgundy Wine: Float shade on the nose.
9. Buttermilk: Stipple lightly on the top of the ears, hands, and feet and top of the leaves.
10. Antique Gold: Float shade on the eyes and mouth and base the cut edges of the eyes and mouth on the pumpkin.
11. Light Avocado: Shade the bottom of the leaves.
12. Brandy Wine: Float shade on the pumpkin under the mouth and around the bear's paws.
13. Black: Dot the eyes and spatter the piece lightly.
14. Outline everything with a permanent black lining pen.
15. White: Spatter the piece.

20

SAILOR BEARS
11-1943 All American Bears

PALETTE:
DECOART AMERICANA

French Grey Blue	Toffee	Buttermilk	Burgundy Wine
Raspberry	White Wash	Sable Brown	Uniform Blue

SUPPLIES:
Black Pen
#1 Round Brush
Stencil 41-5019 Stars/Checkerboard
19 Gauge Wire

WOODCUTTING HINTS: The pieces are cut from 3/4" wood. The overall finished size of the set is 13 1/4" x 8 3/4".

WOOD PREPARATION:
Sand and seal the wood.

PAINTING INSTRUCTIONS:

1. Toffee: Base the bears' hands, legs, feet and heads.
2. French Grey Blue: Base her dress and bloomers. Base his shirt and knickers.
3. Buttermilk: Lightly stipple the center of the face and the feet and tops of the hands. Base the collars, cuffs and hem of her skirt. Line the stripes with a #1 round brush.
4. Raspberry: Dry blush the cheeks. Base the nose.
5. Sable Brown: Float shade on the heads, ears, neck, arms and feet.
6. Toffee: Float shade on the collars, cuffs and hem of her skirt.
7. Uniform Blue: Float shade on the dress sleeves, skirt and bloomers, and around the collar. Shade his pants and cuffs, sleeves and under the collar.
8. Burgundy Wine: Stipple the cheek area again. Float shade on the noses. Water paint down a little and paint the rick rack on with a #1 round brush. Stroke the bows on. Spatter everything lightly avoiding the faces.

9. Black: Dot the eyes.
10. White Wash: Dry brush on the tummies, sleeves, knickers and bloomers. Dot the cheeks and eyes. Spatter everything lightly.
11. Line everything with a black permanent lining pen.

The Flag
1. Burgundy Wine: Base two stripes.
2. Buttermilk: Base one stripe.
3. French Grey Blue: Base the left side.
4. Toffee: Shade the Buttermilk stripe.
5. Cranberry Wine: Shade the red stripe.
6. Uniform Blue: Shade the left side.
7. White Wash: Stipple the center of the red, white and blue areas. Stencil two stars in the blue area. Spatter lightly.
8. Lamp Black: Spatter lightly.
9. Line everything with a permanent black lining pen.

Finish: Wire the heart to the hand with the bears on each side of the heart.

WHICH TREATS?
31-2655 Paper Mache Shopping Bag Set x 3 (middle size)

PALETTE:
DECOART AMERICANA

Antique White	Moon Yellow	Lamp Black	Red Iron Oxide	Light Buttermilk
Burnt Orange	Avocado	Antique Gold	Jade Green	Evergreen
Slate Grey	Toffee	Sable Brown	Raspberry	Burgundy Wine

SUPPLIES: Black Pen #1   19 Gauge Wire (24" cut 4)

PAINTING INSTRUCTIONS:
1. Antique White: Basecoat the entire container.
2. Toffee: Base the bear.
3. Lamp Black: Base the hat.
4. Moon Yellow: Base the cape.
5. Burnt Orange: Base the pumpkins. Base the bow.
6. Jade Green: Base the large leaves on the pumpkins. Float the grass.
7. Sable Brown: Float the bear's head, ears, tail and body. Float around the outside edge of the container and around the bear and pumpkins. Float the cape. Base the stems.
8. Light Buttermilk: Stipple the tummy and toes, cape and hat, top of the ears, and pumpkins. Float highlights on the bow and leaves. Stipple highlights on the container between the edges and the pattern.
9. Raspberry: Base the nose. Dry blush the cheeks.

23

10. Jade Green: Line the grass and stroke some small leaves in the grass.
11. Burnt Orange: Dot the flowers around the edge of the container.
12. Antique Gold: Dot the flowers on the pumpkins.
13. Black: Dot the flower centers. Line the cape with stripes. Dot the eyes.
14. Slate Grey: Line the top of the hat brim.
15. Avocado: Shade the leaves. Base the word "Treats".
16. Evergreen: Line some more grass and stroke some leaves in the grass and the small leaves by the flowers.
17. Red Iron Oxide: Float shade on the pumpkins and bow.
18. Burgundy Wine: Float the nose.
19. Buttermilk: Float the top of the nose. Dot the cheeks. Spatter lightly.
20. Black: Spatter everything lightly.

Finish: Outline everything with a permanent black lining pen. Curl the wire, intertwine two pieces together, then wire to the container.

ARM FULL OF HEARTS
This wood is not available through Provo Craft

½" wood
cut 3

PALETTE:
DECOART AMERICANA

Toffee	Raspberry
Cranberry Wine	Sable Brown
White Wash	Lamp Black
Burgundy Wine	

SUPPLIES:
19 Gauge Wire
Stencil #41-5060 Mini Tweeds

WOODCUTTING HINTS: The bear is cut from 3/4" wood. The hearts are cut from 1/2" wood. The overall finished size is 10 1/2" x 12".

WOOD PREPARATION: Sand and seal the wood.

PAINTING INSTRUCTIONS:
1. Toffee: Base the bear.
2. Raspberry: Base the nose. Dry blush the cheeks. Base the bow.
3. Burgundy Wine: Float shade on the nose and the bow and base the hearts.
4. White Wash: Stipple the ears, muzzle, arms, tummy and feet. Float highlights on the bow. Stencil designs on the hearts. Dot the cheeks. Float a highlight on the top of the nose. Stroke and dot the top of the nose. Spatter the hearts and the bear.
5. Sable Brown: Float shade on the ears, head, around the arms, body, legs and feet.
6. Cranberry Wine: Float shade around the hearts.

7. Lamp Black: Dot the eyes and spatter the bear.
Finish: Outline everything with a permanent black lining pen. Thread wire through the hearts and attach to the hands as shown.

MY FLAG
This wood is not available through Provo Craft

PALETTE:
DECOART AMERICANA

Toffee	Burgundy Wine	French Grey Blue	Sable Brown
Deep Midnight Blue	Cranberry Wine	White Wash	Buttermilk
Raspberry	Lamp Black		

SUPPLIES:
Stencil 41-5019 Stars/Checkerboard

WOODCUTTING HINTS:
This piece is cut from 3/4" wood. The overall finished size is 7 1/2" x 5 1/2".

WOOD PREPARATION:
Sand and seal the wood.

PAINTING INSTRUCTIONS:
1. Toffee: Base the bear.
2. Buttermilk: Base the middle stripe. Stipple the toes, hands and ears.
3. Raspberry: Base the nose. Dry blush the cheeks.
4. Burgundy Wine: Float shade on the nose. Base the stripes on the flag.
5. Cranberry Wine: Float shade on the red stripes.
6. Toffee: Float shade on the White Wash stripe.
7. Sable Brown: Float shade on the bear's ears, neck, face, hands, legs and feet.
8. French Grey Blue: Base the blue square on the flag.
9. Buttermilk: Stencil a small star in the center of the blue square.
10. Deep Midnight Blue: Float shade around the blue square and around the star.
11. White Wash: Dot the cheeks. Spatter the pieces
12. Black: Dot the eyes. Spatter the pieces
Finish: Outline everything with a permanent black lining pen.

27

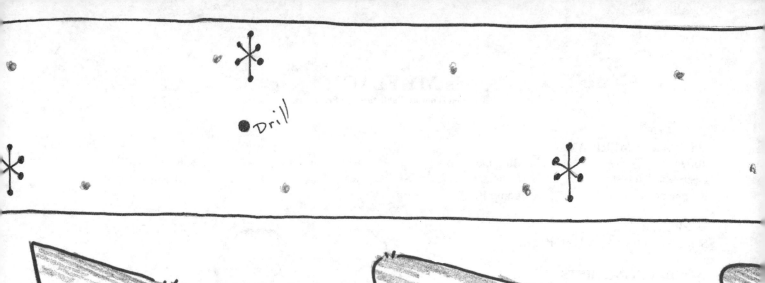

WINTER TIME
11-1948 Wintertime

PALETTE:
DECOART AMERICANA

Hauser Medium Green	White Wash	Plantation Pine	Baby Blue
Raspberry	Burgundy Wine	Lamp Black	Toffee
Sable Brown	Moon Yellow	Antique Gold	French Grey Blue
Deep Midnight Blue			

WOODCUTTING HINTS: The tree, penguins and rack are cut from 3/4" wood. The feet, sign and bear are cut from 1/4" baltic birch plywood. The overall finished size is 17 1/4" x 14".

WOOD PREPARATION: Sand and seal all the wood.

PAINTING INSTRUCTIONS:
1. Hauser Medium Green: Base the tree.
2. Deep Midnight Blue: Base the mitten holder.
3. Black: Base the penguins.
4. White Wash: Base the bear. Stipple the penguins' tummies and dot their eyes.
5. Baby Blue: Base the vest.
6. Moon Yellow: Base the beaks and feet.
7. Raspberry: Base the nose. Dry blush the cheeks.
8. Toffee: Float shade on the bear. Base the winter sign and the fur on the penguins' hats.
9. Burgundy Wine: Base the hat on one penguin.
10. French Grey Blue: Base the hat on the other penguin.
11. Antique Gold: Float shade on the beaks and penguins' feet.
12. Plantation Pine: Float shade on the tree.
13. Sable Brown: Float shade on the sign and on the fur on the penguins' hats.
14. White Wash: Stipple the center of the sign and hats. Dot the snow on the holder and line and dot snow flakes. Dot the vest. Spatter White Wash on the penguins, holder and tree. Stipple highlights in the center of the penguins' feet. Dot the bears' cheeks and float a highlight on his nose. Float a highlight across the top of the fur trim on the penguins' hats.
15. Black: Dot the eyes. Spatter the penguins' feet, the bear, and the sign.
16. Deep Midnight Blue: Line the lettering on the sign and dot the buttons on the vest.

Finish: Outline everything with a permanent black lining pen.

BEATRICE BEAR TOWEL HOLDER
This wood is not available through Provo Craft

PALETTE:
DECOART AMERICANA

Toffee	Sable Brown	Moon Yellow	Buttermilk
Raspberry	Burgundy Wine	Lamp Black	White Wash
Evergreen	Shale Green	Lt. Avocado	

SUPPLIES: Sweet Hearts Stencil 41-0527

WOOD CUTTING HINTS: The bear is cut from 3/4"
wood. The dowel is 1/2" wide and 15 1/2" long. The wood
pieces to hold the dowel are 3/4" wood. The overall finished size is 16 1/2" x 10 1/4".

WOOD PREPARATION: Sand and seal the wood.

PAINTING INSTRUCTIONS:

1. Toffee: Base the bear's head, hands and legs.
2. Buttermilk: Base the collar and border of the dress.
   Lightly stipple the ears, muzzle, hands and legs.
3. Shale Green: Base the dress and shoes. Base the
   dowel and the holders. Line the stripes on the border
   and rick rack on the collar.
4. Sable Brown: Float shading on the ears, head, hands
   and legs.
5. Toffee: Float shade on the collar and dress border.
6. Moon Yellow: Stencil the hearts onto the dress. Line
   rick rack on the sleeves and border.

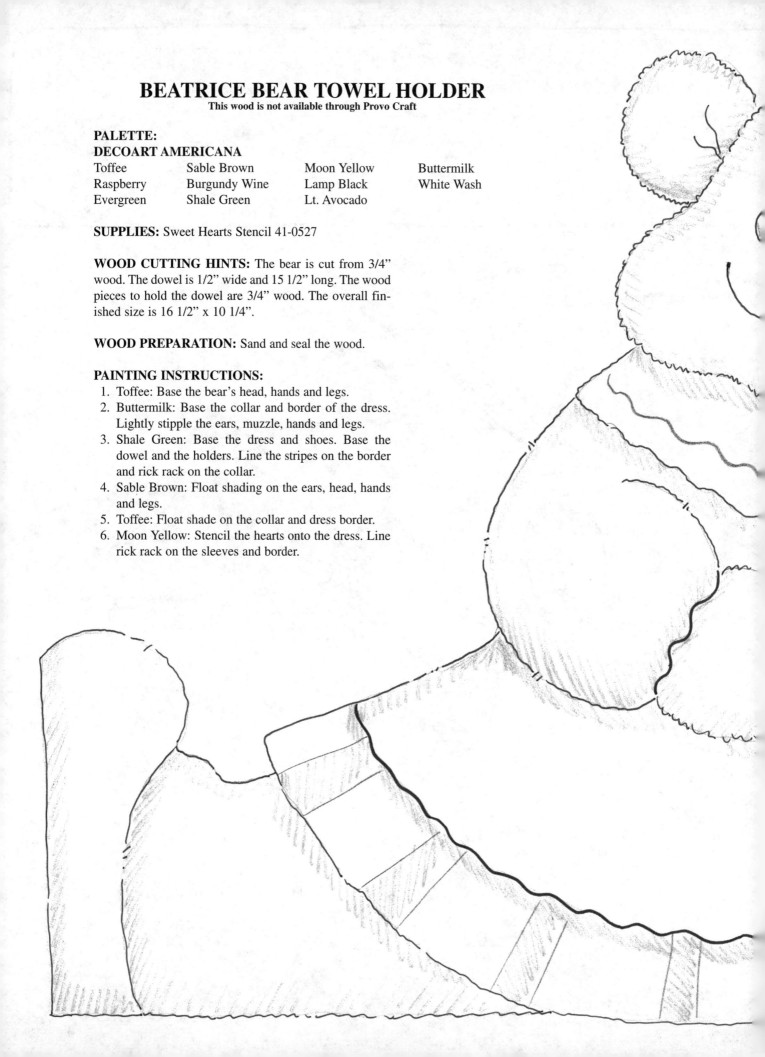

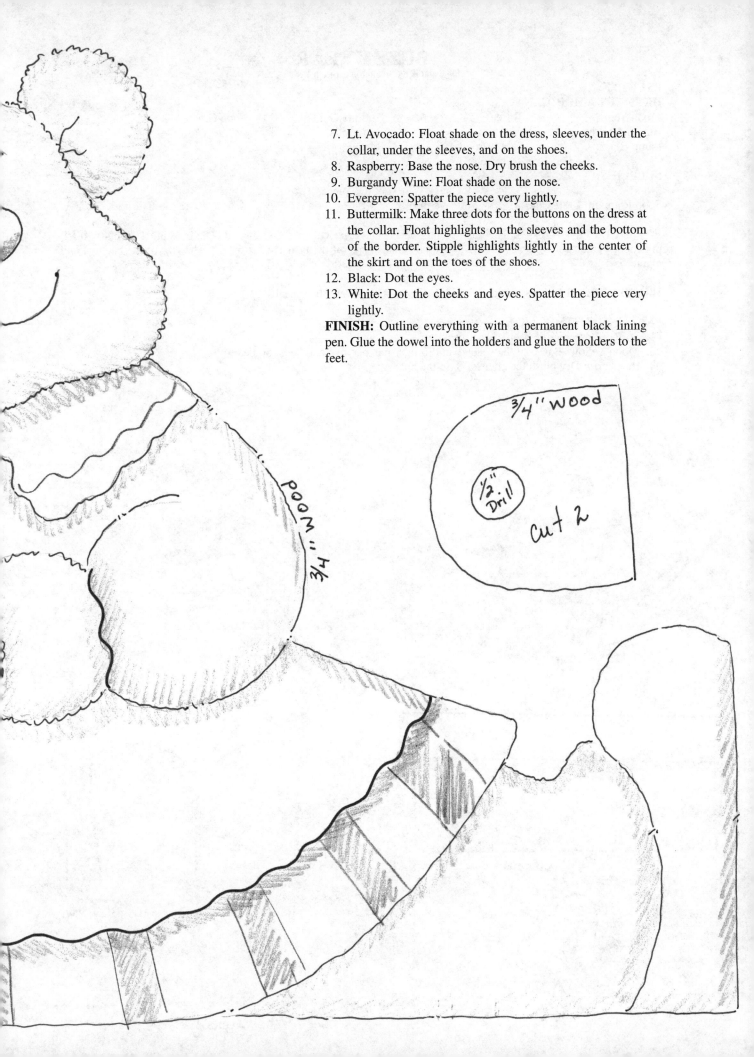

7. Lt. Avocado: Float shade on the dress, sleeves, under the collar, under the sleeves, and on the shoes.
8. Raspberry: Base the nose. Dry brush the cheeks.
9. Burgundy Wine: Float shade on the nose.
10. Evergreen: Spatter the piece very lightly.
11. Buttermilk: Make three dots for the buttons on the dress at the collar. Float highlights on the sleeves and the bottom of the border. Stipple highlights lightly in the center of the skirt and on the toes of the shoes.
12. Black: Dot the eyes.
13. White: Dot the cheeks and eyes. Spatter the piece very lightly.

FINISH: Outline everything with a permanent black lining pen. Glue the dowel into the holders and glue the holders to the feet.

3/4" Wood

1/2" Drill

Cut 2

3/4" Poom

BUZZY BEAR
This wood is not available through Provo Craft

PALETTE:
DECOART AMERICANA

Moon Yellow	Toffee	Antique Gold	Jade Green
Burgundy Wine	Avocado	Buttermilk	White Wash
Lamp Black	Sable Brown	Raspberry	

SUPPLIES:

Moss
Sobo Premium Craft Glue

19 Gauge Wire (cut two pieces 12" long each)
Satin Varnish

WOODCUTTING HINTS: The bear, planter and beehive are cut from 3/4" wood. The bees are 1/8" baltic birch plywood. The dowel is 2" x 3/16". The overall finished size of the bear is 6" x 6 1/2". The size of the beehive and planter is 5" x 4".

WOOD PREPARATION: Sand and seal the wood with a water base sealer.

PAINTING INSTRUCTIONS:
1. Toffee: Basecoat the bear's head, neck, arms, legs, and feet.
2. Moon Yellow: Basecoat the second and forth stripe, beehive and bees' bodies.
3. Raspberry: Dry blush the cheeks. Base the nose.

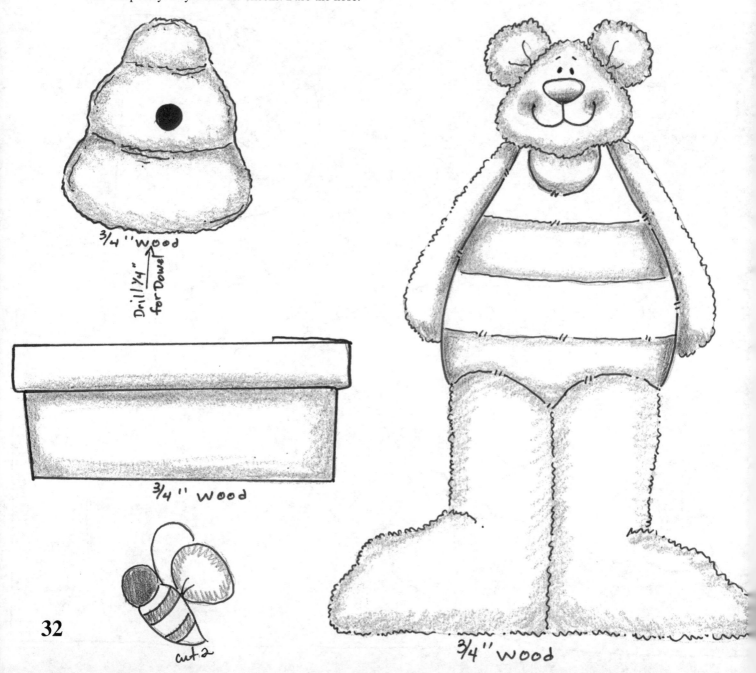

3/4" wood

Drill 1/4" for Dowel

3/4" wood

cut 2

3/4" wood

32

4. Jade Green: Base the planter box.
5. Sable Brown: Float shade on the bear's ears, head and arms, neck, legs and feet.
6. Burgundy Wine: Float shade on the nose.
7. Black: Base the first and third stripes on the bear, bees' heads and stripes. Dot the beehive hole and bear's eyes and mouth.
8. Buttermilk: Base the bee's wings. Stipple the center of each stripe on the bear, and highlights on his legs, arms and ears. Float the top of the nose and dot the cheeks. Stipple highlights on the bees' bodies, the planter and in each section of the beehive. Base the dowel.
9. Avocado: Float shade on the planter box.
10. Sable Brown: Float shade on the bee's wings.
11. Antique Gold: Float shade on the yellow stripes, the beehive, and the yellow sections of the bees' bodies.
12. Black: Spatter lightly.
13. White Wash: Dot the eyes. Spatter the bear.

Finish: Outline everything with a permanent black pen. Use squiggly lines on the bear and beehive. Use a water base satin varnish. Lightly curl the wire to form the wings and glue into the holes in the back. Glue the dowel to the beehive and then to the planter. Glue the moss around the dowel then glue the bees to the planter.

BOB BIRD WATCHER
11-1942 Bob Bird Watcher

PALETTE:
DECOART AMERICANA

Toffee	Buttermilk	Baby Blue	Moon Yellow
French Grey Blue	Uniform Blue	Raspberry	Black
Burgundy Wine	Avocado	Sable Brown	White Wash

SUPPLIES: Moss   19 Gauge Wire (8" long)   Stencil No. 41-5089 Checks, Hearts & Dots

WOODCUTTING HINTS: The bear with bird, birdhouse and base are cut from 3/4" wood. The sign and fence are 1/4" wood. The dowel is 3/16" in diameter cut 7" long. The overall finished size is 8"x 8".

WOOD PREPARATION: Sand and seal the wood.

PAINTING INSTRUCTIONS:
1. Toffee: Base the bear.
2. Baby Blue: Base the bird.
3. Buttermilk: Base the fence. Stipple the tummy, muzzle, feet and arms of the bear. Base the sign and the bottom part of the birdhouse.
4. Avocado: Base the base and leaves. Line the stems and grass. (There is one flower with stem, leaves and grass on each picket as shown in the colored pictured.)
5. Sable Brown: Float shading on the bear, ears, arms, head, tummy and feet, around the fence, birdhouse and sign.
6. Raspberry: Base the nose. Stipple the cheeks. Line the flowers on the bear and the fence. Lightly stipple the tops of the ears.
7. French Grey Blue: Base the bird house roof. Stencil small checks on the sign. Float shade on the bird.
8. Uniform Blue: Float shade on the roof.
9. Burgundy Wine: Float shade on the nose.
10. Moon Yellow: Base the bird's beak.
11. White Wash: Float a highlight on the nose and dot the cheeks. Lightly spatter the bear.
12. Black: Dot the eyes and flower centers. Dot the lettering on the sign. Dot the hole in the birdhouse. Outline everything with a permanent black lining pen.
13. Uniform Blue: Spatter the bear and the fence.

Finish: Glue the fence together. Screw the bear to the base. Curl the wire and attach to the sign. Glue the fence to the base. Glue the dowel to the birdhouse, then into the base. Glue on the moss. Glue the sign to the bear.

• Drill   ● Drill

3/4" wood

cut 1

cut 2

HELLO

34